A COLONY LEADER

ANNE
HUTCHINSON

BY DORIS FABER

ILLUSTRATED BY FRANK VAUGHN

GARRARD PUBLISHING COMPANY
CHAMPAIGN, ILLINOIS

For Nina

Picture Credit: Page 1 Courtesy of
The Secretary of the Commonwealth of Massachusetts

Map by Henri Fluchere

1614845

Contents

1. A Rare Girl

"My brother has hurt his hand," ten-year-old Anne Marbury called out breathlessly. "He fell on a rock, and it cut him to the bone. Quick, hand me a strip of clean linen!"

Will Hutchinson had already stopped his pony cart by the side of the dusty road, for the sight of a girl running down the steep path from the top of Lookout Hill had surprised him. What could a girl be doing in this lonely spot, holding her gown above her ankles and racing like the wind?

But as soon as he recognized Anne, Will was less surprised. Anne Marbury was always doing or saying something unexpected. Besides, she was so very clever with words that although Will was fully fifteen, he couldn't help feeling foolish whenever he tried to talk to her.

Part of Will's shyness with Anne came from the fact that his father kept a shop, while her father was a preacher. In England, in 1601, this made a big difference. But for once, Will was glad to be the son of a storekeeper. As soon as she reached the cart, he offered Anne the finest piece of cloth he had.

"That will serve nicely," Anne said. "Now, do, please, tear it for me. I must hurry to bind Frank's wound."

Poor Will, Anne thought, as she started up the path again, leaving the boy staring silently after her. Why does he never speak? Then she quite forgot about him in her haste to reach her brother.

But Will was still waiting when she came back down the hill, leading Frank by his unharmed hand. Frank was younger than his sister, and not nearly as tall. Because she was such a sturdy girl, Anne had become used to mothering her small sisters and brothers.

"Oh, I am so glad you waited, Will!" she cried out in some relief. "I fear Frank is feeling weak. It would be kind of you to drive him home in your cart."

"I—I aimed to, Miss," Will managed to say.

When they drew up at the Marbury gate, Anne thanked Will warmly. But she did not linger, because she was too concerned about Frank. Again she forgot Will as she ran to summon her parents.

Fortunately, Frank recovered from his fall with no ill effects, and soon all was as usual for Anne. Every day, she helped her mother care for the younger children. She knitted stockings. She studied the Bible with her father.

Anne loved the peaceful little village of Alford, where her family lived. She had been born there, on July 17, 1591, and she had never known any other home. But as the years passed, she sometimes felt sad.

"What troubles you, daughter?" her father asked her one day when she was fourteen.

Anne spoke up eagerly. "I would be so happy if I could only see some other part of the world," she said.

The Reverend Marbury smiled. "I have news for you," he told her. "We are moving to London!"

2. In London

The bustle of London thrilled Anne.

But she spent very little time out of doors.
As the daughter of a respectable family, she
could not think of walking the narrow, crowded
streets alone. Nobody related to a minister would
dream of visiting the playhouse where dramas by
one Will Shakespeare were attracting noisy mobs.
Still, Anne found excitement enough.

Almost every day, friends of her father came
to dine at the Marbury table, and their talk
fascinated Anne.

Religion was the main point of dispute in
London during the early 1600's. People in every
walk of life argued about religion, and even
fought about religion. With her lively mind,
Anne eagerly followed all of the discussion.

Should the old, traditional ways of worship be followed? Or were new ways needed?

It was not considered fitting for a girl or woman to take any part in conversation about such serious subjects. But Anne's father never objected if she drew up a stool and sat listening while one minister after another spoke his views.

Then, after the guests departed, the Reverend Marbury would willingly answer his daughter's questions. No other of his ten children was as keen as Anne, he had already decided. So he fell into the habit of speaking frankly to her about his own religious problems.

Anne already knew some of this story, of course. Even as a small child, she had heard about her father's terrible few months in Marshalsea prison.

"Have him to the Marshalsea!"

That's what an old bishop had commanded, after hearing young Mr. Marbury criticize some practices of England's church leaders.

In particular, Anne's father had disapproved of letting unworthy men serve as ministers only because they belonged to wealthy families. Yet the Reverend Marbury never went as far as some men in attacking the established ways of conducting church services. Even so, he had been forbidden to preach for several years after his release from jail.

Now he was permitted to preach again, but some bishops still suspected him. In truth, the Reverend Marbury was growing more and more discontented.

However, before he reached the point of speaking out openly again, he fell sick and died.

Anne was shaken with grief. "What's to become of me now?" she asked herself. If only it were possible for a female to be a minister! She longed for nothing so much as the chance to take up her father's unfinished task.

But she knew how the very idea of a woman standing up to preach would shock every bishop in the kingdom. So what was she to do?

"You must find a good man, and wed him," her mother suggested gently.

With a sad smile, Anne shook her head. "None would have me," she said. "Who would want a wife who longs to be a minister?"

Anne's mother sighed. Truly, the girl was too clever for most men, that was the trouble. So the years passed, and several of Anne's younger brothers and sisters married. All this while, she cheerfully helped her mother at home. And she spent every free moment studying her Bible.

Then, when she was twenty-one, an unexpected visitor called on her. By this time, Anne thought of herself as an old maid who would never marry. Indeed it was rare for a woman to find a husband after she had reached such an advanced age.

But Anne didn't look a bit like an old maid when she recognized the man standing at her front door.

"Will Hutchinson!" she cried. "Whatever has brought you to London?" And a warm glow of memories from her country childhood turned her cheeks pink.

Her smiling welcome encouraged Will. He was still too shy to tell her how much he had admired her when she was just a little girl. Nor could he tell her how his heart had leaped when he heard by chance that she was not married. But he could say how glad he was that he had dared to make this trip.

Anne was clearly pleased to see him, and soon her simple pleasure in renewing an old friendship changed into a deeper feeling. She married Will Hutchinson in London on August 9, 1612. Then she moved back to Alford with him.

3. "Thine Eyes Shall See"

A pale little girl was asleep on the grass when Anne Hutchinson came out into her garden one spring morning several years later.

"Wake up, child," she said gently. "Have I not seen you at the farm beyond the old mill? Pray, what is your trouble?"

Still rubbing her eyes, the little girl stood and tried to curtsy. "It's my ma who needs you, Mistress Hutchinson," she said. "Ma's down with the fever again."

Mrs. Hutchinson nodded. In the time since she'd returned to Alford as Will Hutchinson's wife, she had grown used to being called on like this. All around the countryside, farm wives thought of her when illness struck, because she

knew so many healing herbs and also because she had such understanding ways.

Even though she had a new baby of her own every year or two, she was always willing to help other families. So she pored over old books till she knew as much about medicines as most doctors did. Because no church would accept a woman minister, she couldn't preach the word of God to heal people's spirits. But at least she could brew potions to heal their bodies.

Still, Mrs. Hutchinson never stopped feeling that religion was the foundation of life. Her faith was so strong that she actually did more than give out herb tea or fever powders. At the farm beyond the old mill, for instance, she saw at once that no medicine could cure the little girl's mother. But Mrs. Hutchinson would not let the poor woman despair.

In addition to doing everything possible to ease her pain, Mrs. Hutchinson also raised her spirits by speaking to her in simple words about God's goodness, and His love for all who loved Him. Whether she knew it or not, Anne Hutchinson really was preaching the word of God as well as practicing medicine.

But in the quiet of her own room, Mrs. Hutchinson's own prayers were more and more troubled. She could never doubt the glory of God, but some of the accepted methods of worshiping Him upset her.

A century earlier, in several countries, feelings like those that were distressing Mrs. Hutchinson had brought great changes. Till that time, all of Europe had been united in the Roman Catholic Church. Then some men had protested against the established ways so strongly that large groups of people broke away from the Roman church and formed new churches.

In England, King Henry VIII founded the Church of England at about the same period when other Protestant churches were being founded. However, he acted purely for personal reasons. When he wanted a divorce which the pope in Rome refused to grant him, Henry decided that church affairs in his country must be controlled by its own king.

But should the services in the new church follow the same pattern as in the old days? What sort of robes should clergymen wear? Questions like these had been stirring bitter arguments ever since Henry's day.

By and large, the other new Protestant churches favored less ceremony than Rome, and they also tried to limit the power of their leaders. In the

Church of England, though, many powerful figures fought to hold on to their privileges. Those who disapproved of this, and felt that a more *pure* form of worship was needed, became known as *Puritans*.

After much prayer all alone in her room, Anne Hutchinson became a Puritan.

Taking this step was no light matter. In many parts of England, Puritans were so hated that they had to hold their meetings secretly. Some Puritan families had moved to Holland, but even Holland no longer welcomed them. More and more Puritans were braving the stormy Atlantic to sail all the way to the wilderness of New England.

Mrs. Hutchinson knew what she was risking when she became a Puritan, but she felt that she had to follow her own conscience. Her husband agreed with her, for he still stood in awe of her superior learning. Week after week he drove her to the nearby market town of Boston.

This was a center of Puritanism. Here there were still open meetings led by the Reverend John Cotton, one of the most brilliant speakers in the Puritan cause. Mrs. Hutchinson listened to his sermons, and her spirit rejoiced. At last she had found the teacher she had been seeking!

But hardly had Mrs. Hutchinson found him when he was removed from her sight. He had finally attracted the attention of London bishops who detested Puritanism, and they commanded: "Keep silent!" The Reverend Cotton would not, and he did not want to go to prison. Instead, he boarded a ship bound for a new Boston far across the ocean.

Then Mrs. Hutchinson sat alone in her room again and prayed for guidance, while her husband and their children waited anxiously outside the closed door. Finally she emerged, holding her Bible in both hands.

It was opened to the chapter containing the words of Isaiah, the prophet. Anne Hutchinson read aloud in her clear and sweet voice:

"Though the Lord give you the bread of adversity, and the water of affliction, yet shall not thy teachers be removed into a corner any more, but *thine eyes shall see thy teachers.*"

Will Hutchinson bowed his head. It would be hard to bid farewell to Alford, to leave his friends and his shop. But he could not stand in his wife's way. If she felt called to follow the Reverend Cotton to distant New England, so be it. He would depart for London at once, to find out when the next ship was sailing!

4. Aboard the *Griffin*

In the summer of 1634, Anne Hutchinson boarded the good ship *Griffin* at a London dock. Her youngest child, baby Susanna who was barely seven months old, nestled in her arms, and little William was tugging at her skirt as they walked up the gangway.

Then came Will Hutchinson with the older children—Katherine, Mary, Anne, Samuel, Francis, Bridget and Faith. Nineteen-year-old Richard was the last in line.

Edward, who was almost twenty-one, had sailed to America some months earlier with an uncle. They were building a house for the family in the new Boston.

Nobody could tell what dangers might lie ahead. Other women, leaving the world they had always known, looked fearful, but not Anne

Hutchinson! The voyage would take only two months, she reminded her family. Then they would be snug and comfortable in their new home.

Yet even a summer crossing of the Atlantic was far from easy, as they all soon discovered. Only a few hours after they set sail, the *Griffin* began bobbing like a cork. The people and the animals aboard became seasick.

For in addition to some two hundred passengers, the ship was also carrying almost as many cattle to the New World. There were no separate compartments for this livestock. So everywhere on deck, babies were crying, mothers were feeling seasick, and frightened cows were trying to pull loose the ropes that tied them to the railing.

Even when the ocean turned calmer, and barrels of food could be lifted out of the cargo hold, the cries of the children continued. They could not be satisfied with the dry salted meat that had been taken along for eating on the long voyage. Soon many of the young ones turned weak and feverish; an infant died, and then another.

Only Mrs. Hutchinson seemed able to preserve a hopeful air. "Trust in the goodness of God," she told the mourning mothers. With her firm faith and her friendly ways, Mrs. Hutchinson spread comfort all day long. Her fellow passengers all took heart from her words—except the two ministers aboard.

The Reverend John Lothrop and the Reverend Zachariah Symmes were both strict and severe in their manner. None among the Puritan passengers wore any but the plainest clothes, and yet these two stood out with their black cloaks and their frowning faces. They listened to Mrs. Hutchinson's comforting words, and they shook their heads.

"The woman dares to preach her own ideas!" the Reverend Symmes said to his fellow minister.

"She must be taught a lesson," the Reverend Lothrop answered.

To them, *obedience* was more important than love. So the next day the Reverend Symmes preached a long sermon warning that anybody who failed to obey the laws of God would be punished severely. He said that no sin, not even a small one, could be forgiven. He also said that the infants who had died aboard the ship were already suffering the terrible torture reserved for all sinners.

Anne Hutchinson listened quietly, but her eyes

flashed sparks of fire. As soon as the Reverend Symmes finished, she hurried to his side.

"Mr. Symmes," she said, "why did you frighten those poor women whose babies died? Will you tell me—"

The minister coldly interrupted her. "Mistress Hutchinson," he said, "it is not fitting for you to question me."

Mrs. Hutchinson's face turned pale, but she spoke up once more. "Surely God loves little children," she insisted. "He knows that they cannot understand many things. If a child dies before reaching the age of reason, God would not punish the child."

Mr. Symmes shook his head. "I warn you, Mistress Hutchinson," he said. "The laws of God have been studied by the wisest men, and you must obey them or you will be sorry." Then he left her before she could say another word.

Mrs. Hutchinson stood a moment deep in thought. Was it for this kind of cruel preaching that she had left the safety of Alford? No! But she could not stay angry.

Her dear Mr. Cotton would never preach this way, she told herself, and she turned her mind to the happy day when they would arrive at the new Boston.

All aboard the *Griffin* joined in joyous prayer on the September morning when land was finally sighted. Even the Reverend Symmes and the Reverend Lothrop wore unaccustomed smiles as they gave thanks for their deliverance from the perils of the sea. But after they sailed in closer to the Boston harbor, the happy excitement faded.

Young Richard Hutchinson spoke up for them all. "I don't like the look of this new Boston," he said disgustedly. "It's nothing but a few little huts made of logs!"

For once, his mother could not urge him to look on the bright side. At her own first sight of her new home, even Anne Hutchinson started to weep!

5. New Boston

Mrs. Hutchinson stopped weeping as soon as she spied her oldest son. Edward was standing in the little throng by the waterside waiting to greet the *Griffin*'s passengers. What a grown man he seemed already! And there was Will Hutchinson's brother beside Edward, and other friends from old Boston, including Mr. Cotton.

The sight of her son and her cherished teacher made Mrs. Hutchinson rejoice that she had dared to leave Alford. Of course, she still missed her tidy home there, and her garden with its neat beds of herbs and flowers. But in the next few weeks she quickly grew used to her new surroundings.

As she soon discovered, all around the new Boston was a tangle of salt marsh and woods.

Out toward some of the other settlements of the Massachusetts Bay Colony, several families had started farms. These could be seen from the hilltops as tiny islands where man had made a mark in the wilderness. But for all its untamed look, this new land had a grand beauty of its own— and Anne Hutchinson loved it.

Most especially, she loved Boston. Though Edward had built just a log cabin, it did provide ample shelter for the time being. Come spring, Will Hutchinson and his sons would build a stronger house, but there was no cause to worry over that matter. Meanwhile, even the biting east wind of Boston's winter did not distress Mrs. Hutchinson.

Here she felt more fully alive than in old England. But almost all of the other women were frightened by the drastic change in their lives. They had to learn how to cook new foods, such as the Indians' maize, and they had to do without the comforts they had always known. Often, they and their children fell sick.

Then Mrs. Hutchinson was always ready to offer help. After cooking for her own family, she cheerfully boiled another pot of soup for an ailing neighbor. She sat up with feverish mothers and took care of their children.

A young woman named Mary Dyer, who had worked as a hat-maker in London before crossing the ocean, became seriously ill after the birth of her first baby. Mrs. Hutchinson hardly slept till both mother and child were out of danger.

"Do you never tire, Mistress Hutchinson?" Mary Dyer asked her.

Mrs. Hutchinson smiled at the question. "Surely I do, Mary," she answered. "But then the Lord gives me new energy."

Besides doing so much to help other people, Mrs. Hutchinson started a new garden in the spring. Then, after her husband and sons had built a larger house, she was busier than ever. Will Hutchinson had sent to England for supplies, and his wife had one of the biggest houses in the colony.

But busy and content as she was, Mrs. Hutchinson had one worry. Ever since she had been in Boston, she had kept it to herself. She was troubled by the harsh tone of some of the preaching she heard in church. Mr. Cotton still made her heart soar whenever he spoke, but Mr. Cotton shared the pulpit with some other ministers.

In particular, the Reverend John Wilson struck her as a cold and cruel man. He reminded her all too clearly of the Reverend Symmes from the *Griffin*, who was now in charge of a church in an outlying settlement.

When she listened to Mr. Wilson she felt a great urge to stand up and argue with him. Yet she could imagine how her own father would have been shocked by such disrespect. So instead she thought of another plan.

6. Mistress Hutchinson's Meetings

One Monday morning, after an especially gloomy sermon by Mr. Wilson, Mrs. Hutchinson called on Mary Dyer, the young hat-maker. And on Jane Hawkins. And on several other women who had been comforted by her own words of faith.

"Will you come to see me this evening?" Mrs. Hutchinson asked in each house she visited. "I would like to talk about the sermon given yesterday."

Six women came to hear Anne Hutchinson that first Monday evening, and a week later *sixty* came. Because so many husbands were curious to discover what their wives found of such interest, Mrs. Hutchinson soon began holding a second meeting on Thursday evenings for both men and

women. Well over a hundred people were present at these gatherings.

What was Mistress Hutchinson up to?

The Reverend Wilson angrily asked the question, and turned even angrier when he heard the answer.

So this woman had the boldness to criticize his sermons!

No, she was merely *explaining* the sermon preached in church the preceding Sunday, her friends insisted.

"She means no harm," the Reverend Cotton said repeatedly.

"Ah, but she *does* harm," the Reverend Wilson answered.

So Mr. Cotton felt more and more unhappy. Not that he himself was completely in sympathy with Mr. Wilson's stern views, but he preferred smoothing over any differences rather than making an issue about them. And he advised Mrs. Hutchinson to do the same.

Now it was her turn to feel unhappy. Would Mr. Cotton truly wish her to go against her own conscience?

No, certainly not, he said warmly.

Then if her conscience told her that she must keep on with her meetings, how could she stop them?

Mr. Cotton sighed. "I fear trouble ahead," he said. And he was right. Within just a few months, the biggest storm in the history of Massachusetts Bay Colony burst over Anne Hutchinson's head.

7. Sound and Fury

"This woman threatens our church!"

"She threatens our state!"

"She threatens both our church and our state!"

In Boston's shops and at its dinner tables, and in every village in the Massachusetts Bay Colony, angry ministers argued this way against allowing Anne Hutchinson to continue her meetings.

Those who said that she was really a double threat—to the established church, and to the legal government of the colony—had good reason for their concern. For Massachusetts Bay was not a democracy during its early days. It was a *theocracy*.

This meant that the church and the state were so closely bound together that, in effect, they made one single governing body. Only Puritans could vote or hold office, and no other religious group was allowed within the colony's borders. On every sort of matter, the will of the church was enforced by law.

For instance, when it turned out that at least some of the Puritan women liked to dress up a bit on special occasions, the strict ministers were disturbed. So they asked the colony's ruling council to consider this question, and a new law was passed forbidding any use of lace to trim a gown.

To the Reverend Wilson and all those who thought along the same lines, Anne Hutchinson's offense was much worse than merely wearing lace.

They sincerely believed that life was a terrible contest between the forces of good and evil, and that most people were too weak to escape being tempted by the devil. So the sternest rules were needed to thwart Satan, rules that everybody had to obey. The Reverend Wilson was afraid of allowing any individual freedom.

Although Mrs. Hutchinson's meetings gave hope and comfort to so many people, even some of her friends could see the danger of permitting them to continue. "If Mistress Hutchinson can say what she wishes, then why can't every Tom, Dick, and Harry hold meetings, too?" they asked.

No, that would surely cause problems, many people agreed.

The young governor of the colony, Henry Vane, and a few other forward-thinking people were much less fearful. They tried to convince their fellow citizens that no real harm would come of allowing free discussion. "Let everybody speak," they said. "A peaceful discussion will help to clear up many issues and make us stronger in the long run."

"Ah, but how can we keep the peace if the ignorant are free to debate with the wisest men?" the Reverend Wilson demanded. "I promise you armed uprisings unless this woman is silenced."

Armed uprisings! The mere words struck terror in many hearts. All through history, there were frightening instances of religious warfare. Could this happen in Massachusetts?

Shivering at the very thought, many good people turned their backs on Anne Hutchinson. They voted against delegates to the law-making assembly who supported her right to speak, and they even threw Governor Vane out of office. They restored their old governor, John Winthrop, to power—and that was a bad omen for Mrs. Hutchinson.

Governor Winthrop hated Vane, and he disliked anybody who was as friendly with Vane as Mrs. Hutchinson had been. So Governor Winthrop lost no time in discussing Mrs. Hutchinson's case with the Reverend Wilson. They decided that the best way to proceed would be to turn the woman's remaining supporters against her. Within the next few weeks, many of them were arrested.

They were charged with being guilty of all sorts of "errors" in their own religious views. But the words used to explain their crimes were so confusing that none of the accused could defend themselves.

Even so, they were punished severely. One minister who had spoken up in favor of Mrs. Hutchinson was banished. Some of her neighbors who had signed a petition supporting her had their property taken away, or lost the right to vote. Then many of Mrs. Hutchinson's former friends changed their minds, and others who still felt that she was right became afraid to say this openly.

Meanwhile, sermons about religious "errors" rumbled down out of almost every pulpit in

Massachusetts. The name of the offending wo-man was on every tongue. But in all the sound and fury over Anne Hutchinson's meetings, one fact was forgotten.

It was the fact that the Puritans of Massachusetts had left England and settled in this new land because they craved religious free-dom for themselves. They well knew how it felt to be prevented from worshiping God in their own way. Still they were not yet ready to do unto others as they wished others to do unto them, and so, on November 7, 1637, they sum-moned Anne Hutchinson into court.

8. The Trial

It was a cold day when Mistress Anne Hutchinson stood up to defend herself before the highest officials of the Massachusetts Bay Colony.

There was no heat in the bare and unlit courtroom. Mrs. Hutchinson had reached the age of forty-six and her health was no longer what it had been. In a few more months she would give birth to her fourteenth child. Yet she stood straight and tall, still giving the appearance of being a woman of great strength.

Governor Winthrop himself opened the case against her.

"Mistress Hutchinson," he said, "you are called here as one of those that have troubled the peace of the commonwealth and the churches."

Every bench was filled with solemn-faced men, and many of them nodded approvingly as Governor Winthrop went on:

"You have spoken many things, as we have been informed, very damaging to the honor of the churches and the ministers thereof."

No sound broke the silence, but the governor's sharp voice grew louder.

"You have maintained a meeting in your house," he said, "and this has been condemned by the general assembly as a thing not permitted, but still you have continued the same."

Governor Winthrop paused, then said slowly: "Therefore, we have summoned you so that we may either rescue you and make you a profitable member among us; or, if you be stubborn, take such action that you may trouble us no longer."

Anne Hutchinson did not turn pale. She knew that she faced being sent away from Massachusetts Bay. That was the punishment for all those who would not be led by the opinions of the leading clergymen. Two years earlier, Roger Williams of Salem had been exiled. Others had suffered the same fate. If it was God's will that she be ordered to leave Boston, then perhaps she and her family might journey southward, to join Williams in Rhode Island.

But Mrs. Hutchinson was not ready to give up her cause without fighting for it. She had neither friend nor lawyer to speak up for her in this court. Governor Winthrop and the Reverend Wilson had seen to it that none of her supporters were admitted. Not even her husband or her sons had been given permission to be present. Still Mrs. Hutchinson felt fully capable of speaking for herself.

During a whole long day, and then another, she did just that. No matter how Governor Winthrop battered at her, she would not admit that she had erred.

"I am called here to answer before you," she told him repeatedly, "but what is the charge against me?"

"I have told you already," Governor Winthrop said impatiently. "What more can I do?"

"Name one charge, I pray you."

Then the governor would confer with the Reverend Wilson, and after a moment inform her that she had sinned by slandering clergymen. Did she not hold the ministers of the colony in error on this fine point, or that fine point, in one sermon or another?

But instead of falling into the trap of disputing with the ministers who testified against her, Mrs. Hutchinson kept insisting on her own right to express her faith in God's goodness.

"What gives you that right?" Governor Winthrop finally demanded.

"That's a matter of conscience, sir."

Then Governor Winthrop lost his temper.

"You must control your conscience," he snapped at her, "or it will have to be controlled for you."

Still the hearing droned on with one black-cloaked minister after another testifying how seriously Mistress Hutchinson had erred. Even her dear teacher Mr. Cotton could not help her, although he tried. Though she meant well, he finally said sadly, it was nevertheless clear that she was misguided.

For two whole days, the proceedings continued, but in this strange sort of court Governor Winthrop was both the chief accuser and the chief judge. His decision could be in no doubt.

Knowing this all along, Anne Hutchinson had still hoped that she might win her case by the simple truth of her defense. Freedom of conscience—that was the principle she was upholding, and sooner or later it must triumph. But its time had not yet come in 1637.

So after two long, cold days in court, Mrs. Hutchinson was sentenced to be sent away from the Massachusetts Bay Colony as a person not fit for the society of decent people.

In an odd show of mercy, Governor Winthrop added one further condition. Because the winter snows would make travel through the wilderness so difficult, there would be a delay of four months in imposing the court's verdict. But during these months the accused was to be imprisoned in the home of some high-minded minister, who would do everything possible to bring her to see the error of her ways.

Anne Hutchinson heard the verdict without flinching.

9. A Bitter Winter

Many times during that winter, Mrs. Hutchinson wished that she had been sent out into the wilderness right after her trial. Surely the worst snowstorm, or even the most savage Indians, could not have added to her suffering. The cruelty she endured in her imprisonment was harder to bear, she thought.

For she was kept during these months in the home of a stern friend of the Reverend Wilson. Neither her husband nor her children could visit her. But a whole host of black-coated enemies tormented her every day.

"Mistress Hutchinson, admit your errors," the Reverend Symmes insisted, shaking his bony finger as if to cast some spell upon her.

"Cease your evil ways, before it is too late," another angry minister warned her.

Though it was clear that her health was failing, they all kept hounding her unmercifully. And yet, by their own lights, they were being kind to her. They truly believed they were offering her one last opportunity to escape the devil.

According to their way of thinking, any person who dared to defy them deserved worse punishment than merely being sent away. Even in the wilderness, this sinner would still be a member of the Boston church, and would thereby be protected at least in some measure from Satan, they reasoned. So, unless she could be led to see how wrong her ideas were, a further step would be necessary. They would have to go through the fearful ceremony of casting her out of the church.

To avoid this terrible step, these ministers kept tirelessly buzzing around Mrs. Hutchinson, and accusing her, and attacking her. Under the continuous pounding, she grew weaker every day. At last, almost fainting with weariness, she finally did admit that she had erred in one respect.

"Doubtless I have taken too much upon myself," she said in a low voice.

"Ah!" the Reverend Symmes exclaimed. "You have indeed been puffed up with a sense of

your own importance. You are guilty of the sin of pride. Now you must beg forgiveness, and be proud no more, woman."

Anne Hutchinson bowed her head silently.

She could go no further. She could not promise to give up listening to her own conscience. No, she must be free to worship as she chose.

The Reverend Wilson was not satisfied. So on March 15th he summoned the members of the Boston church to attend the most solemn gathering ever held in the Massachusetts Bay Colony. Every bench was filled, and among those present this time were some members of Mrs. Hutchinson's family as well as many of the people who had attended her meetings.

But the loyal Will Hutchinson was nowhere to be seen. He had been sure that his wife would be forced to leave the colony. So, with a party of nineteen trusted men, including his own grown sons, he had gone into the wilderness some weeks earlier to search for a place where they could build a new settlement. They hoped to find some suitable land near Roger Williams in Rhode Island.

Among those who did come to the meeting, some had already suffered for supporting Mrs.

Hutchinson. But one man was still brave enough to rise in an attempt to defend her. Before he could speak a word, the Reverend Wilson declared him out of order.

Then the minister coldly called for Mistress Hutchinson to be led in to hear the awful penalty she had brought upon herself.

There were gasps of surprise and pity as Anne Hutchinson walked into the crowded church. Many eyes filled with tears. For the tall and strong woman they remembered had changed sadly during her imprisonment. That she would very soon give birth to a baby was obvious from her slow and heavy step, but her pale face had changed even more than her figure. Lines of pain and sorrow showed how she had been suffering. She looked very ill.

But she stood in patient silence when the Reverend Wilson stepped forward again. Then he spoke.

"Mistress Anne Hutchinson," he said, "in the name of the Lord Jesus Christ, I do not only pronounce you worthy to be cast out, but I do cast you out. . . . And in the name of Christ I do deliver you up to Satan. . . . Therefore I command you . . . to withdraw yourself out of this congregation."

10. Aquidneck

By now, Will Hutchinson had found a likely piece of land in Rhode Island and he was building a log cabin there. And his oldest son, Edward, was hurrying back through the wilderness all alone.

Fortunately, Edward arrived in Boston just in time to be with his mother when the Reverend Wilson spoke his dreadful sentence. Anne Hutchinson leaned on her son's arm as she walked slowly out of the church. All who were present bowed their heads in silence while these two departed.

Not even stopping to rest, Edward then went to gather up his younger brothers and sisters, who had been staying with trusted friends. A dozen of these good friends who could not be frightened out of their love for Mrs. Hutchinson had already decided to join the family in its exile.

"Make haste!" Edward kept urging. He had promised his father to do his best to prevent further trouble from Governor Winthrop.

So they quickly packed only the most necessary food and clothing, no more than they could carry themselves. And they set forth the day after the Reverend Wilson pronounced his sentence.

Mrs. Hutchinson was glad to leave Boston. Though she had spent a few happy years there, she thought that its air was no longer fit for breathing. Until its leaders learned to allow more freedom, she had no wish to see the town again.

As for her being forbidden church membership, she felt relieved now that her own conscience really was her only guide. Let the Reverend Wilson do his worst, she need not worry. Now she could worship God in her own way, and she was sure He would not cast out any who loved Him.

Thus, her spirit knew more peace than it had in many months. But Mrs. Hutchinson's hardships were far from ended. Winter lingered late that year and the travelers stopped to wait

for better weather at a farm kept by relatives outside of Boston, but the air was still frosty when they had to resume their journey.

Because there were no roads through the deep woods they had to cross, they traveled by foot. Weak as she was, for six days Mrs. Hutchinson walked through trackless forest. She slept six nights on the frozen ground. Then when she was close to collapse, they arrived at the Providence settlement started by Roger Williams.

Fortunately, she did not have much farther to go. The place Will Hutchinson had selected as their new home was on a green island the Indians called Aquidneck, not more than a good day's journey from Providence. But when Mrs. Hutchinson arrived at Aquidneck, she hardly had the breath left to greet her husband.

"I fear she will not live much longer," Edward sadly told his father.

Within just a few weeks, Mrs. Hutchinson gave birth to the baby she was expecting. Alas, the poor infant was born dead, and it seemed that the mother would also die. For several months, she was too ill to rise from the rude bed Will Hutchinson had built for her.

During this time, the news of her baby's death and her own illness was brought back to Boston, and Governor Winthrop shook his head knowingly. "The woman is being punished by God for sinning," he said. Even some of her old friends believed him, and shivered.

But as the months passed, Mrs. Hutchinson slowly regained at least some of her old strength, till she could begin taking an interest in this new place the Lord had spared her to see. Aquidneck was amply blessed by nature with a mild climate, and grand rocky cliffs overlooking the blue water. The handful of families who had come there in freedom did not envy any other people anywhere in the world.

Anne Hutchinson no longer felt strong enough to preach to her friends and neighbors, but she took comfort in small meetings at which all present prayed silently, or else spoke in turn if they were moved to do so. By choice, the people of Aquidneck built no church, preferring to hold their prayer meetings in each other's houses.

After several years, life in this untroubled wilderness healed Mrs. Hutchinson's spirit, and she looked forward to growing old peacefully there. Then suddenly her calm was shattered. In the spring of 1642 her dear husband, who was fifty-six years old, became ill. Within a few days, he was dead.

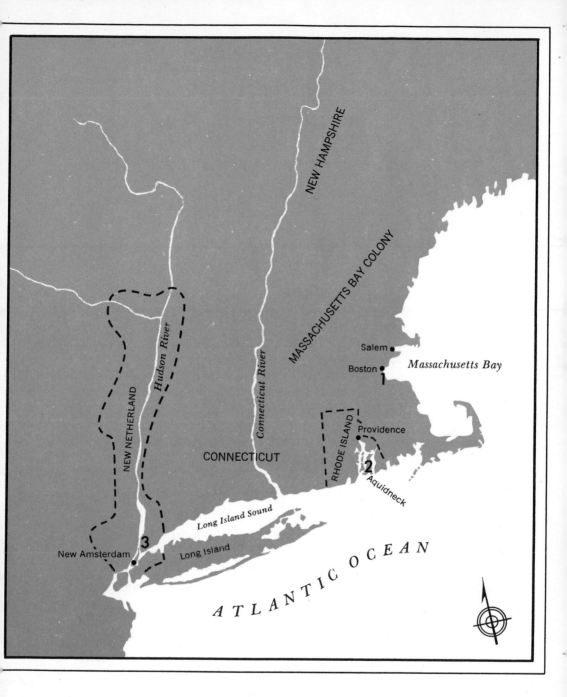

1. Boston, in the Massachusetts Bay Colony, where the Hutchinsons first settled.

2. Aquidneck, Rhode Island, where Anne Hutchinson fled with her family after her banishment from the Massachusetts Bay Colony.

3. Anne Hutchinson's farm on Long Island Sound where the family was attacked by Indians.

11. A New Start

After her husband died, Mrs. Hutchinson would have liked to have remained the rest of her life in the farmhouse he had built. Her older children were already married, and several had settled near her or in Providence. So she had willing hands to help her run the farm and care for the younger children still at home.

She had also found a new interest since regaining her health. A tribe of friendly Indians was taking up much of her attention. These Indians were already living on Aquidneck when the settlers from Boston arrived.

"You must remember that they are savages at heart," Mrs. Hutchinson's sons warned her.

She shook her head gently. "They are God's creatures," she answered. "At heart they are good, not evil."

Believing she could help these fellow men by teaching them something about her medicines made of common herbs, and about her own religious faith, she spent many happy hours visiting with the Indians

But during the months following her husband's death, there were more and more signs that she might not be allowed to remain undisturbed in her wilderness retreat. Since the founding of Providence and other settlements that would soon be combined to make up the colony of Rhode Island, the leaders of the Massachusetts Bay Colony had been claiming that all this land really belonged to Massachusetts.

Because travel was so difficult, not much had been done to back up this claim. However, the existence of a few settlements which refused to recognize the authority of ministers like the Reverend Wilson increasingly struck strict Puritans as a threat. They began sending messengers southward, ordering the rebellious settlers to mend their ways.

When all of these messages were disregarded, Massachusetts became even more concerned. It seemed possible that armed soldiers might be sent out any day, to take over the wilderness area by force.

Fearing not so much for her own safety as for that of her children, Mrs. Hutchinson decided to move still farther to the south.

Below New England, in the Dutch colony of New Netherland, she would be able to worship as she pleased without any interference from Massachusetts. That's where she would go!

Late in the summer of 1642, Mrs. Hutchinson left Aquidneck with most of her family. Thirty-five other Rhode Island families joined her on her new pilgrimage to escape religious persecution.

This journey was longer than her flight from Boston, but less difficult. In fine weather, and with sandy meadow instead of deep forest along most of their route, they were able to drive their cattle easily, and even bring wagons carrying household goods. Much of the time they stayed right in sight of the blue waters of Long Island Sound, which greatly pleased Mrs. Hutchinson, for she loved to look out over the water.

So she was more than happy when the men of the party picked out a tract of land for their new homes bordering on this same calm body of water. Her own farm extended inland to a small stream. None of this area had yet been settled by the Dutch, though it lay safely within their territory. In years to come, it would be called Westchester County, and the small stream would be known as the Hutchinson River.

Dutch officials farther south in New Amsterdam willingly gave permission for the new settlement when several of the men from Aquidneck called upon them. But a serious problem soon arose. On the morning the men returned from New Amsterdam and began chopping down trees to use for building log cabins, Indians with fierce streaks of red painted on their faces gathered on the beach.

These were members of a tribe which had already learned to distrust white men. Other land of theirs had been taken from them without fair payment, and they had been promised that they would not be disturbed in this area. Now it seemed to them that another promise was about to be broken.

So the painted Indians advanced and stood in a circle around the white men who were cutting a tree trunk into logs.

All of the Aquidneck women and children were camped nearby. They saw the Indians

advance, and they saw their own men keep right on working.

"These Indians mean no harm," Mrs. Hutchinson said in her clear voice. Remembering how she had made friends with the Aquidneck Indians, she thought she would do the same in this new place. But these Indians seemed far less willing to accept her friendship.

As she stepped forward, their leader also took a step, and he made signs with his hands that had an unmistakable meaning. Go away, he gestured. Go away!

Then he turned and led his followers back toward the beach, while fearful murmurs arose among the Aquidneck women and children.

"All will be well!" Mrs. Hutchinson said calmly. If only she were right!

12. Unheeded Warning

After that first frightening moment the new community had no real trouble from the Indians for a full year. It seemed that Mrs. Hutchinson was, after all, succeeding in making friends with them.

"They are all God's creatures," she would remind her fellow settlers. "Treat them fairly, and there is no reason to fear them."

Mrs. Hutchinson's youngest child, her daughter Susanna, took her mother's assurances as the simple truth. Even when an Indian brave turned up at their door one day with fierce red paint striping his cheeks—a sight the settlers hadn't seen since their arrival—Susanna teased him into running a race with her down to the beach.

Susanna, who was eight years old, had never learned to be afraid of any Indian.

But many of the older settlers could hardly hide their alarm at the sight of the war paint. From passing travelers, they had heard how some of the Indians in other parts of the Dutch territory had already gone on the warpath because still more of their land had been taken from them. Whole families of settlers had been killed.

Surely this one painted Indian had come intending to give Mrs. Hutchinson some sort of warning that the Aquidneck party faced the same fate. But Mrs. Hutchinson herself refused to believe trouble was coming.

Most of her neighbors could not share her calm faith. They gathered up their families and hurried down to New Amsterdam to seek refuge in the Dutch fort there. So they escaped the terrible wrath of the Indians.

On a cloudless day in September of 1643, a band of Indians swept up from the beach with their faces painted fiery red. In their hands were tomahawks. They went first to the house of an Aquidneck family named Throgmorton, who had chosen not to flee southward. The Indians killed every member of that family, butchered its cattle, and set its house ablaze.

On that same September afternoon they killed Mrs. Hutchinson and her whole family.

Only little Susanna escaped. The Indian brave she had played with took pity on her, and adopted her as his own daughter. Otherwise, burned ashes were all that remained of the whole Aquidneck settlement, and these were soon scattered by the wind. Nobody has ever discovered exactly where Anne Hutchinson met her fearful death.

But she has not been forgotten. Because she made such a brave stand in defense of religious freedom, Anne Hutchinson has come to be regarded as one of the outstanding figures in American history.

The Massachusetts Puritans who cast her out did not see the error of their own ways so quickly. Some, like the Reverend Wilson, even said that Mrs. Hutchinson's cruel death was proof that she had offended God, and they kept on doing all they could to keep other people from following their own consciences.

It took many years before religious persecution ended in New England. During those years, others besides Anne Hutchinson suffered for daring to worship God in their own way. Mrs. Hutchinson's young friend Mary Dyer was one of these. For preaching the new Quaker doctrine, which was very much like the religious ideas Mrs. Hutchinson had been working out all by herself, Mary Dyer was hanged in Boston by the Puritans.

Then as the years passed, Boston learned to value freedom of religion as highly as political freedom. Although Massachusetts had banished Anne Hutchinson from its borders, it came to be very proud of her. Now a grand statue of her, holding her Bible in one hand, and leading a little child with the other, watches over the front entrance to the Massachusetts State House.